PAPER SHREDDERS

Danny,
We thought you would enjoy this commingling of your two passions.

Love
Mom & Dad
12-25-05

PAPER SHREDDERS

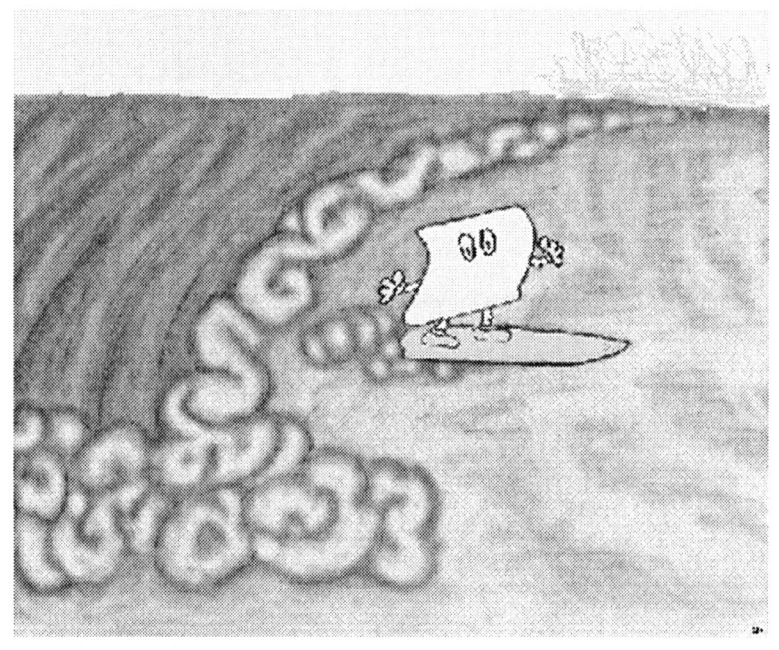

♦

An Anthology of Surf Writing

Edited by
G. Murray Thomas & Gary Wright

iUniverse, Inc.
New York Lincoln Shanghai

PAPER SHREDDERS
An Anthology of Surf Writing

Copyright © 1993, 2005 by G. Murray Thomas

All rights reserved. No part of this book may be used or reproduced by any means, graphic, electronic, or mechanical, including photocopying, recording, taping or by any information storage retrieval system without the written permission of the publisher except in the case of brief quotations embodied in critical articles and reviews.

iUniverse books may be ordered through booksellers or by contacting:

iUniverse
2021 Pine Lake Road, Suite 100
Lincoln, NE 68512
www.iuniverse.com
1-800-Authors (1-800-288-4677)

ISBN-13: 978-0-595-35131-2 (pbk)
ISBN-13: 978-0-595-79833-9 (ebk)
ISBN-10: 0-595-35131-X (pbk)
ISBN-10: 0-595-79833-0 (ebk)

Printed in the United States of America

CREDITS:

Front cover photo of Brandt Bacha by Jason Kenworthy

Title page illustration by Don Lambert

Photo of Gary Wright by Flame

Photo of G. Murray Thomas by James Brewer

PREVIOUS PUBLICATION:

These pieces were originally published in these places:

Surfing, by John Carmona: *Surfrider Foundation South Bay Newsletter*

The Last Wave & Those Who Surf, by Max Montgomery*: A Collection of Surf Stories*

Ten Feet, by Terrence E. Dunn: *Verve*

Kelea of Maui, by Ward Smith: *Local Magazine*

We Surf, by Lawrence Schulz: *We Surf* (FarStarFire Press)

Contents

Introduction xiii
    G. Murray Thomas
- *One of Those Day* *1*
    John Moritz
- *Ho-Dad Haiku* *2*
    John W. Hart III
- *Wordsurfing* *3*
    Mauro Monteiro
- *We Surf* *5*
    Lawrence Schulz
- *Smooth* *8*
    Stephen Kraft
- *Beyond* *9*
    Robert Meyer
- *Untitled* *11*
    Zack Sherertz
- *Bahamian Passage* *12*
    Bob Moseley
- *Kelea of Maui* *16*
    Ward Smith
- *Those Who Surf* *18*
    Max Montgomery
- *Tribe* *20*
    Sebastian Debovian
- *Surf Bums* *22*
    Richard Nester

- *The Surfer* *23*
  Lawrence Schulz
- *Sizes* *24*
  Terrence E. Dunn
- *Surfing* *26*
  John Carmona
- *Cartoons* *28*
  John Moritz
- *Long Days of Devereux* *29*
  Gregory J. Schell
- *A Ledge* *31*
  Terrence E. Dunn
- *Wave to Death* *32*
  Stephen Kraft
- *Liquid Catacomb* *33*
  Steffan Bryce Saidenberg
- *Miramar* *34*
  Kevin Joy
- *Born on the Wind, Dead of 'Humanity'* *35*
  Ryan Korinke
- *Our Debt* *36*
  Sebastian Debovian
- *Plastic Baggies* *38*
  Terrence E. Dunn
- *Ten Feet* *40*
  Terrence E. Dunn
- *Punchy Bouncy* *42*
  C. Mulrooney
- *Risky Cliffs* *43*
  Christine Trzyna
- *Elementary* *45*
  Stephanie Mood
- *My Husband Takes Up Surfing at the Age of 38* *46*
  Charlene Goldman

- *Surfing at 40* 47
  Lawrence Schulz
- *A Big Day, a Middle Aged Man and the Pier* 49
  Don Hurzeler
- *Surf Board Time is Coming* 52
  Stephen Kraft
- *Quenching a Soul* 53
  Terrence E. Dunn
- *Bali Reflections* 59
  Gregory Schell
- *Jalama* 61
  Mike Fraley
- *The Last Secret Spot* 62
  D.J. McNamara
- *The Last Wave* 66
  Max Montgomery

Bios 69
About the Editors 75
- *My Very First Wave* 77
  John Moritz

Paper: noun: A thin flexible material which is written upon.

Shredder: noun: A surfer of exceptional talent [Slang]

Paper Shredder: noun: 1. A machine used to destroy paper (cf: Watergate and Oliver North). 2. One who shreds on paper; ie: a writer of exceptional talent.

Introduction

This book started when, as a poet newly transplanted to Southern California, I discovered the connections between surfing and poetry. I met poets who wrote about surfing, and surfers who were poets.

But the connections went much deeper than that. Surfers and poets approach life in amazingly similar ways. They both live for experience. They both find joy in the possibilities life has to offer. Most important, they both find the meaning of their lives in something other than, higher than, the usual materialistic pursuits of our culture. Surfers and poets define themselves as just that, not by their jobs or what they own. Surfing and poetry are their lives.

One difference is that surfers are happy with the experience itself, while poets feel the need to capture that experience in poetry. Yet within this difference is another connection. Poetry, with its metaphor and ability to express the inexpressible, is the ideal medium for capturing the experience of surfing. Conversely, surfing is nearly impossible to express in writing except through poetry. They were made for each other.

Thus *Paper Shredders* was born. Published by my newly formed Orange Ocean Press, it was conceived as the first of a series of poetry anthologies about "unpoetic" subjects. Other titles in the series included *Polluted Poems* and *Kill the Opossum*, and a never realized volume about laundromats. *Paper Shredders* was certainly the crown of the series.

Due to limited resources and distribution, *Paper Shredders,* in its original Orange Ocean Press publication, is nearly impossible to find. Today, twelve years later, the opportunity to reprint through iUniverse arose. Both editors are pleased that this wonderful anthology of surf writing will now be able to reach the audience it deserves.

We hope you enjoy these surf writings as much as we have.

G. Murray Thomas

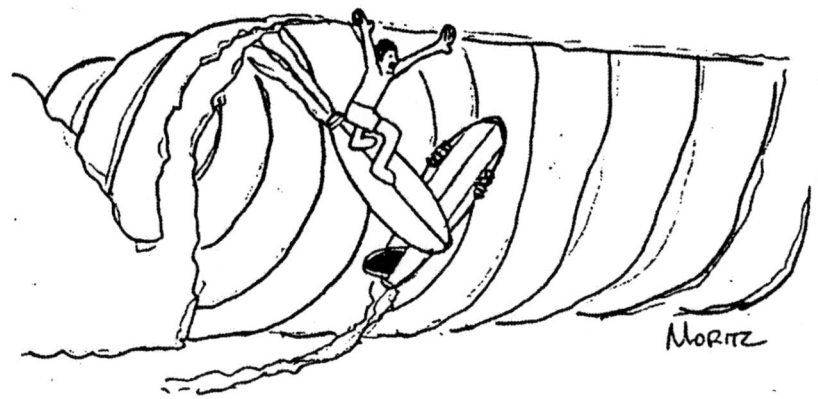

Have you ever had
One of those days
The waves are good
And plenty of rays

You've got a new board
But before you can shout
You get run over
While paddling out.

HO-DAD HAIKU

John W. Hart III

Sliding down the face
Be in control of nature
for one split second.

WORDSURFING

Mauro Monteiro

Alright!
Stop that moment in time!
That was your hardest move
Your cleanest move.

So, was it just another wave?
Locked in a gyration or was it
Clearly a standout in a detailed
Progression of turns in a liquid arena
You were lucky enough to take part in?

Could you have hit the lip any harder?
Or just you think you could glide
Float direct move you tanned and strong
Along through amongst over with…

You were in control, yet a second or so
You let nature take the reigns
And pilot this flight.

Nobody even saw it!
Maybe your buddy did,
But the image was yours
And maybe the day's.

The sun was out.
Witness!
Can I get a witness?

The wind was out, just enough,
And blowing in just the right way…

The sand was there, still and deep
Underneath your tracks...

And the water!
Yeah, she held you, elevated.
Although always beneath her
You knew always as a friend
But more like paper under the pen
Of a scorned lover
And deliberately taunted!

And the water...
Holding you still in time
Holding lessons waiting to be
Put through practice, waiting
To be glassed onto your psyche,
To be poured over your skin.

Alright!
Stop, and think of that moment!
That slash and remember
How close it felt to the moving,
The pushing of gravity
And time...

Sun, wind, sand
And water...
Rising
Over you.

Pulling you
Together.

WE SURF

Lawrence Schulz

There are some of us
For whom
The wind is more than
A meeting of systems.

There are those of us
For whom
The clouds are more than
An accumulation for future rain.

There are those of us
For whom
Our lives are more than just happenstance.
More than just a fast race leading nowhere
On this mad march toward money.

There are those of us
For whom
Our lives mean more
Than possessing things that will trap us.

There are those us
For whom
The waves
Are silent cliffs of water
Meant to cradle us.
To carry us away.

              We Surf
Because each wave is different, has its own power.

            We Surf
Because each wave brings its own rhythm
            We Surf
Because there is this aloneness
We find together here
            We Surf
The names the Wedge, Blackies, Anderson Street
Mean something only to us.
            We Surf
Because we know no other way to live.
            We Surf
In memory of those who have surfed before us
And will never surf again.
            We Surf
For there is no freedom that exists except this freedom
            We Surf
Even away from the water
We carry this ocean with us
            We Surf
We are wave cowboys on an ocean rodeo
            We Surf
Go anywhere, anytime for that one ride
That will stay in our souls
            We Surf
Because we can't think of any reason not to

There are those for whom the ocean
Is a religion that brings us together.
And the water of the waves is the church
That brings us home.

    We surf…
        We surf…
            We surf…

SMOOTH

Stephen Kraft

SIDESLIPPING LIKE A RUG BEING PULLED OUT
FROM UNDERNEATH YOU
CAUGHT SUDDENLY LIKE A TYCO RACE CAR
IN THE SLOT THRUST FORWARD AS IF GOD'S
HAND CONTROL WAS SQUEEZED TO THE HILT
STILL IN DISBELIEF THAT YOU'RE NOT KISSING
THE REEF FEET BELOW YOUR FEET
NOT EVEN AWARE THAT
YOU'RE TOTALLY COVERED
IN THE CAVITY OF THE PACIFIC'S MOUTH
SOMETHING LIKE A CAR CRASH HEAD ON
ROLL OUT SCRATCHLESS YOU RECOVER
& THE FRACTION OF A SECOND IT TAKES
TO ROLL OUT FROM UNDERNEATH
THAT CRUSHING CURTAIN
YOU CAPTURE YOUR SUCCESS OF GLORY WITH
A TRUE GRIT SMILE FROM THE GUY CAUGHT
ON THE INSIDE WHO IS GETTING POUNDED
AND SHOULDN'T BE SMILING
THIS IS SURFING.

BEYOND

Robert Meyer

dig into the froth
paddle through bars of white
heavy waters pass over me as
I disappear beneath a crashing wave

reach the outside
beyond the breakers
beyond the chaos

my mind clears as the morning
anxiety drowns in the winter water

waves emerge from the horizon
dig, dig…
take off atop a steepening face
carve right…all my weight right
and I glide over a wave of glass
as it shatters behind me

feel so in control

stall

the wave feathers over me
a tunnel of water
see its beauty
from the eye of the curl

the tube caves in
taking me with it as it falls
crushing me
oceans hand crushes me

holds me down as it roars
I reach the surface gasping
my lungs burning

the ocean
the ocean
where I have felt invincible
yet frail

Untitled

Zack Sherertz

A warm thundershower…
Fall, falling…washing summer away
Retaining hot-season air
South mix swells come strong, cold winter juice
Transition…
Our suits grow
As our bodies tolerate
Extreme conditions
We…surf…

Wet sunny salt air in our lungs
Stemming from the swift offshore
Taking it all in.
The Amtrak passes
Set wave
Muted hoots
All the way to the beach
Cobblestone rock trot
Sunset while dressing
Green flash?
Summer surviving mosquitoes chase me up the trail.

Bahamian Passage
Bob Moseley

Ordinarily I'd never light a fire inside a house. This time I had no choice, the electricity was out.

It was raining hard, the wind whipping through the covered porch. I brought the hibachi in the kitchen doorway and torched the coals. The smoke floated out the open door and raced around the corner, shaking the palm fronds as it turned into wind, and rain.

The others were in bed. They wouldn't smell, or taste, the occasional wisps that filled the kitchen. If I didn't cook the grouper filets they'd be rotten by morning. Everything in the refrigerator would spoil. If the storm ended right now the current wouldn't be back on for some time. The power lines on the outer islands are always the last to be fixed.

Elbow Key barely runs seven miles, its width never more than three quarters. To the west lie large sounds with dredged canals running through shallow reef and shoals, beginning the interior islands which form the Commonwealth Nation of the Bahamas. To the east, the Atlantic, open ocean, where swells travel for thousands of miles before grooming to vertical, crashing walls along the islands' barrier reefs. From the air, Elbow Key looks like the brow of a human skull, with two rounded bays serving as eye sockets, Hopetown Harbour to the north, White Sound to the south.

We're leaving in three days. Our two weeks almost up, my questions nearly answered, my dreams, my fears, within my grasp.

The grouper steaks were done but I left them on the grill. My stomach had an acid nervousness enticed by too much coffee and the violence whirling in from the ocean, circling the house once or twice, then whipping out across the harbor. The others wouldn't be awake until morning; they had been drinking rum since early afternoon. They wouldn't eat the fish either. We speared them on the reef yesterday. I felt obligated to eat what we took, but couldn't.

It was after we harvested the fish, and were walking along the low road beside a cluster of moored sailboats that we first heard Tropical Storm Erin was definitely headed our way. The Captain of the Sea Duce used his radio to confirm what we all felt, and the locals all knew, was about to happen.

Erin was supposed to skirt by approximately 70 miles due east of the island. Her strongest sustained winds were 60 mph, not quite hurricane force. But even if she were a category 5 storm, the deadliest, there was little we could do. Where could we go? Another island? Why bother? The locals have long since decided to die at home.

But Erin was no killer. By tropical standards she was a mere annoyance, something to keep you in port a couple days, something to make you close the front door for the first time in a week, something to make rain, and wind, to shove 15-20 foot swells reeling like thunder across the reef, something to suck the wind offshore after it passes, brushing the surf clean and glassy, almost innocent and inviting.

My stomach turned sour the second her course was confirmed. In less than 24 hours, years worth of questions would be answered, fears quenched, or brought forth into truth. The dream, and wonder, would be dead, conquered by man or nature, glowing in reality, festering in defeat.

I've waited 16 years to face a challenge that'll be over in seconds. A mere hint of time that means nothing to anyone, except me. Win or lose, everyone else will remain the same. My kids will still love me, my wife will still bitch when I surf too much, my boss will keep looking over my shoulder. Only I will move on, the thrill, or agony, forever part of my soul.

We get fairly large surf on occasion in Florida, but never the surging power that exists only on small bodies of rock, covered with seeping, sandy soil, surrounded by reef as they sit unprotected from the open ocean. No continental shelf slows the wave speed, dragging on it for miles until it's reduced to a fraction of its original statue. Storm swells get so big on the islands they look easy. From the beach riders seem to move in slow motion as they drop into triple overhead faces. You can count one, two, three, four, five, before the rider hits bottom and makes his first turn. From the beach, it almost looks boring.

But perched on the top of a rolling, breaking peak, faced with only an ounce of time to pull back or drop in, it's like riding an avalanche. To over commit, to take the wrong wave, in the wrong situation, can send you free falling into the pit, drilled by the lip and pinned on a living, urchin infested reef, five feet below the surface. Flinch for just a click and you're too far behind, destined to get pitched, thrown out by the breaking curl, sent to a similar fate on the ocean floor.

Years of repetition have given me the instincts needed in tight confrontations, the ability to act, not think; to know you can make it, or at least have more than a fighting chance. This level breeds confidence. You push yourself in sections you'll never make. It just means next time will be easier. That's the only way to surf big waves, without fear or regard. You respect what can happen, even worry about it on the beach, or paddling out. But when you're rising up the face of your wave, stroking to match its speed, you can't think of failure, or fear. You have to know you'll make it, even if you don't.

But sitting in the open doorway, watching the rain and grill, fanning errant trails of smoke from the kitchen, I didn't feel the confidence. I've pushed the limits before, stretching my ability, my nerve. The stakes have been intense at times, like jumping off the pier into the face of Hurricane Diane, or riding the tube over a shallow rock ledge in Palm Beach, or surfing a quarter mile offshore in a northeaster, alone, with no one in sight, in the water or on the beach. I've paid my dues, but the price has never been this high.

I didn't need any more coffee to stay awake, but I poured another cup anyway. At three in the morning, it tastes too good. It went very well with the homemade bread from Vernon's store and the thick real butter I'd never eat at home.

I had given up on the radio. The batteries were dying so it couldn't receive any more stations from Florida, some hour and a half by plane. Earlier that night, after the others had gone to sleep, I found a Spanish speaking station out of Miami. The name of the city was the only word I could understand.

Something in the way the D.J. spoke scared me. There was no music. Just the thin static of A.M. radio and the fast, nonstop, almost panicked gait of his voice. He talked as if there were a national emergency, even though Erin was not affecting the mainland at all. His apparent urgency, I was sure, spilled anti-Castro propaganda, or a calling of the Haitians to arms in downtown Miami. His voice pierced the quiet that only a violent wind can make, building an air of doom inside myself, a fear of the unknown. For a few minutes I understood the feeling of complete hopelessness and lack of control over one's fate that leads man to religion, placing his entire being in the hands of another, so he never worries again; or as an alternative, commits suicide.

I had no real reason to be afraid. It was like the storm, and the radio, the forceful winds, rain, and the thundering surf, opened my vulnerability, waking its existence.

I felt alone, even though my wife and three others slept in the same house. The sudden rattle of tin roof strips blowing down a brick alley bolted me up right, ending my trance-like stare into the glowing coals.

I couldn't stay inside. I walked along the high road a few hundred yards, passing a purple two story house that seemed to be constructed in half portions so it could fit in the tight lot squeezed between the church and a stand of coconut palms. I turned down the cement walk by the church, whose altar stands thirty feet from the ocean. It's protected from the sea by the large coral head on which it sits.

I stood at the top of the small cliff where the head meets the water and looked down the beach. I watched huge rolling waves that had passed the 3/4 mile barrier reef which kills all but the largest of swells. If you see sizable waves there the island's southern reefs are guaranteed to be three, maybe four times as big.

The wind was still blowing, but not as hard. I guessed Erin was moving quickly and would soon pass, pulling the winds along its tail, causing offshores that will carve clean, glassy lines from the confused chop created in the fury of the storm.

I knew in the next hour or two, a little before first light, the momentum would change, all that had been blown shoreward would rest, for a moment, then rock gently while the offshores picked up, chasing the storm away. The palms would straighten, only to be bend over in the opposite direction from the night before. The lizards, and birds, would move to locations uninhabitable just hours before. The clouds would move out, the sun would shine, and the world would seem a different place.

The only remnants of the storm, the wind and rain, would be scattered fronds and puddles, old branches and coconuts, lost yard ornaments, and the merciless lines of power, reaching for the sky before shaking the very foundations of the island itself.

I turned and walked past the church, back to the house, knowing it will soon be done. Today I step to the next level, a higher experience that can never be taken from my soul, or I falter, my dreams rotting in the ooze of my open abrasions.

Either way, the waiting is over.

KELEA OF MAUI
A Surfer First
Ward Smith

Kahekili ruled the kingdom of Maui and Lanai from 1415 to 1445. Kahekili had a son named Kawao and a daughter named Kelea. Growing up in a royal household and having only to compete with her brother, Kelea was handed everything on the proverbial silver platter. She was spoiled beyond belief and of course she was beautiful. As she grew up, men from miles around competed for her affection. As a result of all this attention, Kelea had an attitude. She was wayward, volatile, and capricious, and had no respect for policy (sounds like a surfer to me). She would not accept proposals from any of the chiefs who wanted to marry her. She loved only the water and became the best surf-swimmer in the kingdom. She really liked to surf big waves which scared her brother. She was so graceful and daring that those who watched her believed she was the friend of the water-god.

In 1445 Kawao, her brother, was crowned king. He wanted Kelea to marry a specific chief to better consolidate his kingdom. Kelea stated her surfboard was her husband and she would embrace no other. Furthermore a voice said in the anu at the feast of Lono that Kelea would meet her husband while surfing.

Meanwhile on Oahu, a chief named Lo-Lale desperately needed a wife. His brother was king and only had daughters and was counting on Lo-Lale to marry and have a boy who would eventually become king. As a suitable wife could not be found on Oahu, Lo-Lale sent Kalamakua, his cousin, to other islands in search of one. They agreed that if the woman brought back was not suitable for Lo-Lale, then Kalamakua would marry her.

Several days later, Kelea was having an outrageous session at her home break called Hamakuapoko. After a raging barrel that encouraged hoots from the home crowd, she noticed a canoe invading her spot (this problem has been going on for at least 500 years). She paddled over to see who it was (and probably to shout: "Go home!") and she discovered strangers (non-locals). Of course, one of the strangers was none other than Kalamakua of Oahu. He immediately invited her in the canoe for a fast and furious ride to the beach. Kalamakua then paddled out and took Kelea for a second ride. He was obviously a very skillful canoer. While paddling out for a third ride, they came upon a squall. The ocean raged and they were pushed way out to sea. When the winds finally stopped, they were not in sight of land. When they finally reached land, they landed on Oahu, thanks to the devious navigation of Kalamakua. He immediately hit Kelea with a marriage proposal for Lo-Lale, hoping Lo-Lale would refuse so he could marry her. Unfortunately, Lo-Lale fell immediately in love and courted her so well she consented to marriage. After the wedding, they moved inland to Lo-Lale's home (look out!).

Kawao sent a messenger on to Oahu to find out what had happened to his sister. After meeting with the messenger, Kalamakua went back to Maui to explain the situation to Kawao. Kalamakua was very tactful and Kawao accepted his explanation.

As the years passed by Kelea had three children. Lo-Lale was a wonderful husband and provided Kelea with everything. With everything she needed, Kelea still became restless, bored and unhappy. She really missed the ocean and surfing (here it comes). She longed for the days of her youth when she surfed almost every day. Lo-Lale sensed her restlessness and dissatisfaction and could feel Kelea slipping away. The only joy she experienced was on her visits to the coast where Kalamakua lived. There she spent hours in the ocean. Her visits to the coast were not enough and finally Kelea left Lo-Lale.

When Kelea arrived at Ewa, on the coast, she found a number of chiefs and nobles surfing the excellent conditions. She immediately borrowed a board and paddled into the lineup. Of course her stylish moves excited everyone in and out of the water. Before long everyone was raving about a beautiful woman who had beaten all the chiefs at surfing. Kalamakua, knowing who it was, went over to greet her. After hearing of her problem with Lo-Lale, Kalamakua told her of his promise to marry her if it didn't work out with Lo-Lale. Immediately she agreed to the proposal, and lived and surfed happily ever after.

THOSE WHO SURF

Max Montgomery

Often I find it difficult to explain to others just who surfers are. There are so many different kinds of people and personalities out in the lineup that I can't even describe them all. However, I can describe two main types of surfers: Real Surfers and Hell Men.

First of all, it must be said that Real Surfers don't eat quiche. They are not Republicans. They oppose offshore oil drilling and vote accordingly. Real Surfers belong to the Surfrider Foundation and give generously. They don't litter and actually pick up trash on their way off the beach. Real Surfers know how to read a satellite picture and own a weather radio. Real Surfers live to surf, and surf to live. Real Surfers have spouses who understand this or they are single.

Real Surfers surf because they must, not because it is a job and a way to earn money. Real surfers know who Tom Blake is and think of him as a hero.

Real Surfers have earned respect in the lineup but don't forget to give it to others as well. They are friendly to new faces in their lineup and when visiting other spots. Real Surfers remember that they too once could hardly sit on a surf board and don't hassle beginners. Real Surfers don't drop in on you. They are courteous and actually give you a wave every now and then. Real Surfers hoot at your rides and tell you how far back in the barrel you were. Real Surfers are a pleasure to surf with.

Hell Men are everything Real Surfers are and more. Everyone who surfs secretly wishes to be one. They are the stuff that legends are made of. They are in a league by themselves. They are in the Majors while Real Surfers play Triple A.

Hell Men surf places with names like Dead Man's, Scar Reef and Shark Point. They think booties are the things that babies wear on their feet. They think a squid lid is the top to a jar of pickled calamari. Hell Men surf in the frigid north coast waters in farmer johns. They are not afraid of sharks, but sharks are afraid of them. Hell Men are still wondering what all that fuss was about twin fins and thrusters, as they still tear it up on 7'6" single fins. Hell Men own a least one surfboard that is longer than 9 feet, and it's not a long board.

Hell Men are willing to drive 2 hours up the coast on the off chance that an uncrowded spot will have waves. They are out of the water with plenty of waves by the time you roll out of bed to crack it on dawn patrol. Hell Men don't have stickers plastered across their board; they prefer tattoos. Hell Men go left at Waimea. They also ride it at night. Alone. Hell Men find spots like Nias and Garagagan too crowded, and instead, surf uncharted parts of the world. Hell

Men usually don't work, but if they do, they work 60 plus hours and still surf more than anyone else. Hell Men aren't hooked into the latest surf lingo and don't say things like "oh, dude, that was such an awesome wave, it was, like, so gnarly." They say things like, "Hey, Ed, you could have driven your camper through that barrel with room to spare."

Quite simply, Hell Men don't wear plaid.

When you're out in the water, try to spot some Hell Men and Real Surfers. It is rare to find genuine Hell Men in the lineup, and it's also difficult to fine Real Surfers as well. It hasn't always been that way. Look around and think about it.

TRIBE

Sebastian Debovian

I am one and many,
a collection of figurines
bobbing over each swell,
faces impassive
a mirror of my own.
There are no voices,
tools for those
confined to land,
just the rumble of waves
the cackle of sea birds
as the chill of the ocean
sucks vitality from our limbs.
Sea lions bark at our intrusion,
sneer at our rubber coats
but we have no words,
exclamations are limited to a vertical drop
over a watery ledge,
calm under the pitching veil
or a restless edge
trailing a fan of spray
like an echo.
Words are powerless here,
we sit like a secret,
a puzzle to those on safe ground
who speculate and label;
explanations coming so easy.
Out here,

we are together,
alone.

Surf Bums

Richard Nester

They've been out there for days,
the lovers cutting class,
the loopy-headed guys on their boards,
the blonde bored ones not bored now—
rapt—stoned
on the long suck
and sigh of the cold sea,
reading its big book with their blood.
Had the cosmos not been
this deeply, genuinely, gorgeously
lazy to start with,
what then? Nothing. No Big Bang,
no egg, no semen, no giddy birth,
no salt dawn, not this set (its liquid, striding legs),
neither this breath nor the next one.
So you think surfing is just like sex.
Well maybe it is.
Remember the way you hurt for it
at fourteen, falling into
and out of balance: the night had never
been colder, the river has never been warmer.
What they want from the curl
is just that little piece
of death that lasts forever.
All the names of all the birds
burn in their eyes.

THE SURFER

Lawrence Schulz

Awkward waves
           zig-
                  zagging
between
           wood
                posts,
earth lungs
                breathing.
This dichotomy
he sees:
           The shore;
           The wave; The sea.
A denominator,
uncommon…unnamed.
Part of a fraction,
indivisible…
                non-fragmented.
The surfer holds each
wave to its excess;
they repeat the last true words of this world:
                hush…
                      hush…
                            hush…

Sizes

Terrence E. Dunn

Outside on the point an old man sits
on his ancient 9'6" longboard.
Inside younger surfers—
the youth of today—
slash away fiercely
at small sectiony waves
with painted up ultra shaped thrusters—
all about six feet.
On my beach chair I sit
and watch the show
while my wet suit undampens a bit
and my hair dries to a fine brittle.
To my right
young girls in smally clad bikini tops
sit on the hood of someone's pickup
and smoke cigarettes.
To my left
a thrityish old surfer,
also a longboarder,
sits in his car
eating his wife-packed lunch,
his hair combed back and still wet.
It's the middle of the afternoon
and still the water is filled
with seal-like humans
trying to get away from automation,
trying to get away from civilization,

trying to find themselves,
or anything.

I hear birds,
I hear seagulls,
I hear cute young giggles,
I hear hard rock blaring,
I hear the surf pounding itself
on the rocks,
and the rocks giving and going,
bouncing along with the surf,
always a substantial part of it.
Cigarette smoke filters before my eyes
and I wonder how someone could break
the perfectness of this place,
of themselves,
by striking a match
and lighting up.
But then again,
to each his own
I've always thought.

And the old man on the long board
just caught a huge one,
and the scrumpets on the inside
sat on their boards
and watched
jaws open
as his true knowledge was shown.
To each his own,
to each.

SURFING

John Carmona

Surfing
is the soul

it fills our
hearts
with ecstasy

it fills our
mind
with destiny

it fills our
body
with creativity

but most of all
it's the
essence of our

        spirituality

The ocean
cleanses our
city wounds

the sun
evaporates all our
problems

the bowl ride
transcends
us.

The feeling is

    Alien

to those
who can only
look out of their
window of life

to see
us.

Surfers will

NEVER...
    Expire

from this
world
because they have...

    SOUL

Johnny finds his New Year's resolution, to be kinder and more tolerant in the water, being severely tested.

To the dismay of other, Johnny never learned to go left.

LONG DAYS OF DEVEREUX
Gregory Schell

Standing atop the windswept cliffs of Isla Vista's Devereux Point, the lone, straggly-haired surfer looks upon the mighty blue Pacific and ponders over the nature of existence. As the orange-yellow sun slowly dips below the horizon line, and the wind blows the ice cold water droplets from his earlobes, Griffin stares out into the blue-green ocean waves as they roll to the shore. Like Whitman's young Adam facing west, Griffin wonders at the sight of this vast, abysmal sea, with its decadent Channel Islands and its white-capped kelp beds, and thinks to himself, "How absolutely amazing is this landscape and how many have stood here before relishing its beauty?"

Just then, another lone surfer catches a wave and rides it to the shore, gracefully weaving his way down the green, back-lit wall of water. Griffin, still clad in his all black neoprene wetsuit, sets his board on the white gravel-like sand, and sits down. The wind continues to whip his wet hair across his forehead, and with such inner peace, Griffin just observes, in a Zen-like fashion, the movement of the birds flying across the incandescent sea. As Griffin sits in meditation, a feeling of desolation comes over him, but one that brings him spiritually closer to his soul. "Surfing is truly soul cleansing," he mutters to himself.

Griffin spots two teenage boys scurrying down the trodden pathway, jumping over rocks and branches, hurrying out to catch some early evening glass-off waves. "I used to be just like that," he thinks. "After junior high, racing to my local break just to get in some last few waves before the night creeps in." As Griffin sits some more, the night activity begins to percolate all around him. Down the beach a group of healthy partygoers begins to light a bonfire. As the wood crackles and that distinctive mesquite aroma fills the air, the first sounds of Bob Marley begin to pulsate from some far off apartment. "This is complete perfection," Griffin says. "I'll bet it's all the same experience...whether you're a Taoist sitting on top of some shrouded, misty mountain top, or perhaps a fisherman on the lakes of the Oregon backcountry...it's all the same inner peace...empty mind, one with God, or whatever you want to call it...it's just indescribable." As he looks up, Griffin notices the elongated clouds, screaming endlessly across the sky, somehow alerting us to the imminent end of the day. "Why does everything have to be so final, so ever changing, so that any feelings of peace are sadly interrupted by moments of chaos and confusion?"

As the bicycles cruise by the path, many of them surfers carrying boards and speaking of the waves they caught, Griffin begins to think of a large burrito and a hot cup of coffee that would cap off the whole experience just right. "I wonder if people who live in Tavarua or Fiji have these feelings all of the time?" ponders Griffin. Suddenly the wind picks up a more furious pace, sending the two teenage boys' hopes of glass-off into a choppy nightmare. Each wave breaks with its spray of a thousand irridescent water particles whipping off the top. "Looks like some uncharted, rugged Northern California spot right now…with its bitter cold water and murky visibility…reminds me of Santa Cruz in the winter," Griffin reflects. Soon the last lone longboarder exits the water and Devereux becomes empty, with the exception of a few spooky jellyfish, scouring the area with their ghostlike compositions. "I wonder if the jellyfish know the meaning of life, and we as humans are all just completely lost," Griffin says as he strokes his two week old goatee. "I've figured out that this is really the only time I get to be alone with nature…completely unmediated nature…no television, no photographs, not even my favorite surf mag…just me and nature…I mean, the only thing between myself and the wave is a flimsy piece of styrofoam and fiberglass resin!" Griffin thinks. "In fact, very flimsy judging by the two pressure dings on my tail…damn!!"

By now the sky has turned a purple-black color and the lights from nearby Isla Vista have illuminated the skeleton-like, eroded bluffs that hold up the meager, dilapidated apartments. Griffin, still in a quasi-mystical state, still sits, perhaps watching the dwindling remnants of an earlier bonfire fade away.

"Boy, I wish I could summon a servant who could bring me that burrito…or maybe three fish tacos and a few cold Coronas…and my acoustic guitar…that would be epic," Griffin says. By and by the sands of the hourglass tick away and Griffin sits up, gathers his board and gets his beach cruiser ready for the arduous journey back to his apartment. Griffin takes one long last look at the now black, ominous Pacific, and thinks, as he rides off towards civilization, "What a great thing it is to be alive…really alive!!!!"

A LEDGE

Terrence E. Dunn

Tomorrow I'll be out in the water
When dawn descends bringing
The quiet reminder of immortality
There I live, I survive, I balance on a ledge
Wobbling always, I wait for time to go by
I fall off
I swing back up
I completely overshoot it
I don't know if it is balancing
Or falling
Or living
Maybe that is best
Just nothing, just now, just here
Just being

WAVE TO DEATH

Stephen Kraft

THE COOL GREENNESS BLUENESS FROTHINESS
FLUIDNESS SOUPINESS CARVINESS DEEPNESS
TUBULAR GLASSY WAVE THAT PROPELS ME
ON MY JOURNEY TO THE LOVELY BEACH
WITH THE BEAUTIFUL WOMEN WHO BASK
IN THE SUN FOR FUN
I MAKE A SHOW AS I GO LOVING
THAT WAVE TO DEATH
THANK GOD FOR THE NEXT ONE

Liquid Catacomb

Steffan Bryce Saidenberg

descend these sacred walls of foam
escape the liquid catacomb
hearts of stone weren't made to float
hide from truth, you've missed the boat

young man sells his very soul
he yearns the dawn, the sun's bright knoll
he knows the sea is not his own
the world is his the surf has shown

ocean size is how he feels
toward the sky his body kneels
follows his shadow to the water's edge
into the liquid and over the ledge

the sea is its own infinity
the feelings within will set you free
leaving the world behind on the shore
he heads for the horizon and searches for more

Miramar

Kevin Joy

Blue water stretching
around the point
soon to be orange sky.
Million-dollar houses watch
with pink window eyes.
Waves fold me in their arms,
respite from a confused land
turned aside at the shoreline.
For a moment the sea releases
the freedom and the promise.
Finally in the water again.

BORN ON THE WIND
DEAD OF 'HUMANITY'

Ryan Korinke

Isolated, far from land,
A fierce gale drives a small ripple
Into a forceful swell,
A reckless surge of power to cross an entire ocean.

The swell rambles onward dutifully
To the lucky surfer's exact location
So that he may become united with it
And experience its unique heaviness.

The rider courses on ecstatically,
In the silk sheet smooth barrel,
Protected, as if concealed
In the womb of the mother ocean.

Often it is like this for all,
And they return with gratitude their thanks,
Except for the disrespectful, uncaring
Villains of life who rape the helpless ocean.

They clothe the vulnerable sea
With disgusting ebony sheets,
And feed her, to her discontent
Their superfluous odds and ends.

Our Debt

Sebastian Debovian

Listen to her bellow,
pound the earth with a fluid fist.
Mother Ocean is irate,
splitting surfboards
and bursting blood vessels.
Rolling hillocks of water
slam the beach,
rush up the sand
and grab the ignorant
roughly by the ankles.
Young gladiators
stumble from her clutch,
water draining from their bodies
like failed courage.
Safely above the maelstrom,
I search for the cause
of this blustery temperament.
My eyes rest on water line
encased in plastic
and styrofoam,
the awards of progress.
Careful to avoid her fury,
I scoop up the refuse
gaining armload
after armload
in minutes.
Friends work next to me,
tourists
and children join.

We labor,
clean and scour
our image from her flawless skin,
hoping for forgiveness
from she who we
have forgotten.

Plastic Baggies

Terrence E. Dunn

Bright, hot, sunny, unbelievable out today.
My face feels hot, my chest feels hot,
my legs, my feet, the tops of my eyelids,
everything feels the serenity of the sunny day.
Out within sight are large to medium sized
churning, pitching, and occasionally shapely waves.
Earlier, about two hours ago, I dropped
into a left four footer.
Before I hit the bottom
I started to drop my left hand,
holding on, clutching for dear life,
against the side of the wave.
Without realizing it,
I put myself right in the barrel.
Immediately my peripheral vision
caught the sight of the thick lip
as it slapped itself over my entire body.
It closed down,
my left hand grabbed,
my board was part of my body,
and all of me shot through like a bullet.

When I got off the wave
I looked down at my left hand,
the hand that had just
pulled me into my happiness,
and saw a plastic baggie
stuck to it.
I must have grabbed it

at some point
off the wave.

Ten Feet

Terrence E. Dunn

One year ago I was down in Central America
surfing and finding and looking and believing
in the freedom of myself.
Ten foot high waves that I stood perched upon
brought me back down to earth.
Ten feet up,
perfectly serene with the ground.
Ten feet up,
completely in touch with the dirt.
Ten feet up,
ten feet to a heaven
that I'm not sure exists,
that I truly believe doesn't exist,
yet ten feet up
and there
and in it
and feeling and knowing
that if there is such a thing
as heaven
that I was in it
right then.

One year ago I was back east
marching against the men in their playtoys
that were roaming the streets.
Ten feet up the young GI's
sat on their thrones.
Ten feet before,
ten feet high in their toys.

Were they feeling it
at that moment?
I hope not—
for you
and for me.

Punchy Bouncy

C. Mulrooney

As if I didn't know
man
what the fuuuuuuuuuck
it's all about
it's my surfboard dude
there's something about it
it goes on forever
and the girls
the girls just like it
anything that moves
man, you know?
It's like, wow
the sun comes up
and I'm in the water.
Waves waves waves
keeping afloat
all the way to
the beach.

RISKY CLIFFS

Christine Trzyna

I look back from time to time,
stopping to catch my breath on the way up
a steep beach cliff.
I want new perspectives.
I see passionate waves thrashing over terrible rocks.
I search for the opening of
    the secret cave rumored to
be full of True Love crystals
But I can't find it.
A cove of perfect shells and sparkling sea glass?
All I find is industrial garbage.
Everything seems more rugged and beat up now
Including me.
I have traded my bachlorette bikinis for
One piece spinsterhood.
The sunscreen of past experiences
    didn't protect me from you.
After you I needed a Baptismal
    blessed fresh water healing.
I needed honest white sea foam
    to purify the black sludge of
Resentments.
But when the Spring comes—
When the breeze ripples sails and hats
And the blooming yellow coreopsus
cling lovingly to the hillsides
The way I clung to you after coming-
I miss you.

My feelings are panting dogs,
>   begging recognition,
Dropping driftwood memory sticks at my feet.
I hunt purple urchin shells
Stranded in tufts of sea grass.
The kelp beds waver slightly as you did
>   when you first
Revealed yourself to me.
From those risky cliffs, those troubled rocks,
I watch you surf on twinkling eye waves.
Till the tugging moon drains the gold away
Leaving silver tidepools of hope.
In the charcoal endings embers glow.
I can smell our love like barbecue smoke
>   soaring high above
Everything,
Wending its way up the crevices of the canyons.

ELEMENTARY

Stephanie Mood

You come in big
and high from the beach
though your shoulders are small
your arm is in place around the red board
and your orange swim trunks are
just where they properly should be
but I know the way your ass curves
soft as a sea mollusk
the line I trace with my finger
reaching under, coming to the tip
and the foam of the wave.

You come in dripping with saltwater
a thousand kisses riding home.
You swim in on your feet like whales
spinning weightlessly off a piece of air
a shaft of light, off the shoulders of the sea.
Down below, it is magical there
and I know the world of the fish and curving grass
billions of hidden stars, I've seen them.
I've kissed you, too, because you come in
because our eyes are watering each other
and our lives are naked together in the air.

My Husband Takes Up Surfing at the Age of 38

Charlene Goldman

Newly christened by the sea,
craving epiphany,
he steals off on his swift kelpie.
If mermaids whisper calling him a dawn
he does not say.

Old songs surface warming bones.
Old roads washed out.
Healing.
Freedom from old routines.
Deepening sense of belonging to the chaotic sway.

Blessing him with seafoam, neoprene,
    surfboard wax,
the swaying, seaweedy, briny baptistery cradles him.

SURFING AT 40

Lawrence Schulz

While men my age wait
for their circle
to become complete;
I let the waves break over me,
lost between
this savage baptism of water
and blessed forgiveness of rain,
hearing the words rush/crush
sound-out my surroundings.
The undertow
shows I am nothing
in the force of true nature,
and my breathing is the life-death border
that separates me from ocean species.
Lets me know that here
I am a momentary intruder
to the world beneath the waves.
Now a wave-waiter
I, meant to walk
in the sea of oxygen
while my sea brethren
are meant to glide
through their lives effortlessly.

A seductress song in this
wave motion as I succumb.
No matter how long I leave her…
she finds me.
Her waves slap

this business suit consciousness
away and here
I learn
There is no such thing as youth,
There is no such thing as age
the distance between years
is no greater
than the distance
between waves
to the ocean's rhythm.
I find the wave to ride again,
my circle becomes complete.

A Big Day, a Middle Aged Man and the Pier

Don Hurzeler

For years I have been coming down to this pier to surf. When the surf is building, I am a mixture of afraid and excited, and filled with anticipation. The paddle out is the biggest change since I was a kid. My new short board and my old weak arms make it a long haul out to the lineup.

I always get here early when it is big. I don't mind the crowds that develop later in the day. People tend to stay out of my way. They probably think it is dangerous to be in the same wave with an "old fart" like myself. Most days I have to surf early so I can get to my office on time.

A big south swell means the current will pull you directly into the pier, if you let it. It means the bottom will be churned up making the surfing area look like a mud bath. Rip tides will be clearly outlined by the same discoloration.

Surfing a big south swell at the pier is a rewarding, thrilling and stupid thing to do. The power of the ocean is beyond description. I've been tossed around like a toy, held under the surface until my lungs are ready to burst and generally beaten to a pulp. On the other hand, the second most fun I've ever had has been in a big south swell. I'm hoping for the latter to be true again today.

I'll start my paddle out in just a minute. I wish my wet suit was dry and didn't have so much cold, wet sand in it. I wish I could find some wax. I wish someone else would show up to go out with me. I really wish I were back in bed. Now that I have run through my wishes, I pick up my board, run toward the water and launch myself toward the lineup.

The sun is nearly up and it begins to redden the mist and fog to the east. My heart is pounding from the short run and the underlying fear. Now is the time to paddle like a son of a bitch out to the break.

The side current tugs hard at me. It wants me out of this nice, safe channel and into the fun zone. I point my board half away from the pier and half out to sea.

Damn, it breaks a long way out when it is big! I have never paddled this hard in my life. My arms are so tired that I can barely lift them. My back is cramping up and my heart continues to pump for all it is worth. I keep telling myself that I am having fun.

I continue to flail my arms into the water. My mouth is now so dry I can't swallow. I am breathing as fast as I can and still need more air. My neck hurts from holding my head up off of my board. To hell with the pain, I'm going to make it outside.

Once I reach the surf line, I finally get to rest. Waves are breaking off to my left and I am barely out of the white water. Outside a good-sized set is forming and I turn to paddle again. I paddle hard up the face of the first monster and finally poke through the wave just as it starts to feather. The offshore wind blows the water back onto me like a cold shower. My head hurts from my first soaking of the day. I feel like I've just eaten some ice cream too fast. I'm beginning to look forward to my hot tub at home.

Now that I have made it outside and over the first really big wave, it looks like the next one is going to get me. I sure hope it breaks soon. I don't want to go over the falls backwards on this beauty. It breaks, but almost on top of me. I try to roll under the wave and it grabs my board away. I'm driven to the bottom and put through the spin cycle. When I claw my way to the surface I am surprised to find my board, broken leash and all, just a few yards away. I immediately do my Mark Spitz imitation and reclaim my board.

Once back on the surfboard, I just lay there with leaden arms, diminishing spirits and an awful feeling that I am now positioned right in the middle of the break.

Within thirty seconds, a new set heads my way. There is no way to get over it. My best chance is to turn, paddle hard and try to catch the first and smallest wave of the set. If I fail, the second or third wave will get me and grind me up. I don't think I can take another beating.

I turn and stroke hard. The wave picks me up and the acceleration is terrific. The drop is nearly vertical and I wish I had my old gun so I could creep back a couple more feet. As it is, I'm barely able to keep the nose out of the water and I have almost no control. When I finally do gain control, I get it all. This is my wave. There is a rhythm, a oneness that few things in life can match. I ride it all the way into the shore break, pulling out at the last moment. Hot damn it feels good!

There is never a question in my mind about going back out. I'm too pooped to pop and I couldn't top the last ride anyway. I pick up my board and dash over the sand and trash into the shower.

The sun eventually burns the fog away and the wind calms down. It is warmer now, especially with my wetsuit still on. The beach shower feels great. A quick trip to the donut shop will restore my strength. Now I can return home, happy that I controlled my fear once again. I rush home to tell my family and neighbors

about how I tore the place up...how I showed those young kids how a real man surfs the pier on a big day.
    I love it!

SURFBOARD TIME IS COMING

Stephen Kraft

SURFBOARD TIME IS COMING
& I WILL SHOW MY STUFF
IT'S BEEN TWENTY YEARS NOW
I HAVE CRIED WHEN PADDLING OUT
THE BIG DAYS SEPARATE US,
THE BOYS FROM THE INSANE
I TROMPED THROUGH INDONESIAN COW PASTURES
SEARCHING FOR ULUWATU AS WE WALKED
THRU THE THICKET TO THE CLIFF
CONSISTENT SETS OF 20' SURF ROLLED IN
& CHRIS' "OH SHIT" MEANT SOMETHING
HE WAS ONE OF THE BOYS AND I WAS INSANE
NOW I WAIT FOR MY NEWLY SHAPED SURFBOARD
TO VENTURE OUT INTO THE SURF
& SHOW 'EM WHAT I GOT
ALTHOUGH I WILL EAT SHIT A LOT
AFTER A WHILE ABOUT A MONTH
I WILL FUCK YOU UP
I WILL ROCKET OFF THE BOTTOM & BLAST OFF
THE TOP SLIDE INTO THE PIT UNDER THE CURL
& AND RIDE OUT THE TUBE
& AND BLOW YOUR MIND THINKING
GOD STEVE CAN DO THAT

Quenching a Soul

Terrence E. Dunn

Purely felt, without thought. That's how it was yesterday; that's how it was this morning; that's how it is now. I'm alive again. Hell, I'm warm again. My body down to the cells in my toes—my legs, my chest, my hands, my hairs—everything is warm. Yes, life is once again good. How long has it been since my last one?

Let's see, I took off at nine in the morning LA time and I took a shower before I left. Then I flew all day and all night through God knows how many stops, layovers, refuelings, plane changes, and flight delays, and miraculously ended up in Peru at six the following morning. (I won't even try to add in the time changes. What with going east to Miami and then west and south to Peru, hell, I'd need an algorithmic calculator to figure it out.) After finding my way out of the airport with my bags that actually showed up—unbroken, unscratched, and well, to tell the truth, I was just surprised as shit that they even got there—then I went and surfed all day.

Of course, first we had to make a stop at Umberto's house. He's the surf guide I thought I wouldn't even need—except, of course, for rides to and from the airport. What did I know, huh? Then we had to make the customary four (bare minimum of four) stops along the way to the beach. You see, according to Umberto, and I guess that means all the rest of the Peruvian surfers for that matter (un-surfers I'm not sure of since they were all smart enough not to go to the beach when it happens to be fifty degrees outside, with no chance of sun or warmth for at least two or three months), it seems that stops are not only necessary, but mandatory on the way to any beach. Even if you don't need anything! I think it has something to do with the atmospheric changes that occur on opposite hemispheres. To them, it's normal to make constant unimportant stops. To us (north hemispherians) it's unnormal. Hence the equator…I guess. I figure I'll have to go to Australia next to test my hypothesis.

Anyhow, we finally made it to the beach. It was a left point called Huaico, and without giving my tiredness a second thought I surfed the whole rest of the day—on some nice six to eight footers. My first wave was beautiful eight footer with an unseeably long left wall. I made the long, deep drop, let out a scream, and even before I made the bottom turn and started to climb the face of the wall that would be in front of me, I knew that all the traveling, all the hassles, all the headaches—everything—was worth it. This feeling can't be patented, can't be explained. You can't get this wave in California—not just like this with two people out at a great rocky left point break that was still glassy at one in the afternoon. Yeah, you read me right: still glassy. And it would stay glassy all day. You see, according to Umberto we could surf at six in the morning, ten in the morning, four in the afternoon, or high noon, and it was always be the same way: glassy. That's why you'll often hear surfers saying the mythical phrase, "There are always waves in Peru."

Oh, and in case you haven't figured it out yet, that's also the reason Peruvians can screw around and make a million stops on the way to the beach. They know the waves will "always be there." I'm not positive, but I don't think the word "choppy" can translate into Peruvian Spanish.

So anyhow, where was I? Oh yes, I was talking about the last time I took a shower. Well, after surfing that day I was planning to take a shower at the "hotel" (I'm using that word very, very kindly here) that I was planning to stay at the whole time I was in Peru. Christ, how stupid could I be? I should have known that something was wrong, very, very, very wrong—when Umberto had to convince the "innkeeper" (who was technically a kid—maybe fifteen tops) to open up the "hotel" just for me. Me alone—no one else was there. But he did open it up, and I did walk right in, thinking that it was all quite normal, as normal as glassy waves at four in the afternoon on any day in Peru. And the rooms were okay too. Livable, you know, nothing fancy. Okay, not even close to fancy. Actually, the word "fancy" should probably not be used in the same sentence as this "hotel". Hell, the word "fancy" should probably not even be used in Peru for that matter. Does it translate? Wait, enough of this, I was talking about my "room" and how okay it was. Which it was, I guess…

I had a double bed complete with Alpaca blankets (which later that night I would thank God for), a night stand, a lamp, and just about a foot and half of room around the bed so that one might be able to do the things that one likes (and usually has) to do in one's "hotel" room. Such as: get into bed, get out of bed, walk into the room, walk out of the room, walk to the "bathroom" (I'll get to that later), walk away from the "bathroom", and of course the normal clothes changes, which varies greatly depending on one's idea of "normal" in that situation.

There was also the "bathroom". At least they called it a "bathroom" (or at least bano, which in my many, many, ah…months of Spanish I learned meant bathroom), and it sure looked like a "bathroom". You know, it had a shower, a sink, a toilet, and the obligatory foot and a half of room between everything. Well, almost. But the problem was once you got past the looking and got on to the actual using of one of these fine "bathroom" pieces. There lay the problem. I guess when you ask for a room in Peru, you not only have to ask for a room with a bath, but also a room with a bath where everything works. Which will probably cost you more. Travel agents have a tendency to forget about these little and vital tidbits of information.

So anyhow, I took my freezing cold wetsuit off, after surfing in the freezing cold ocean, and planned on getting into the not-so-freezing shower. I stood there naked and shivering and turned on the faucet. And then I waited…And waited…And after a very, very, very, long minute or three a drizzle of water started spurting out of the shower head. Coughing out of it was more like it. Maybe even burping or belching. But whatever it was, it was definitely not streaming or flowing or any of the other shower-water-type terms you usually associate with a situation like this. It also wasn't warm. Not even close. Once again "warmth" was another of the many words that could not be mentioned in the same breath as this "hotel".

Thinking that maybe, possibly, hopefully it might warm up in a few minutes, I let it "run" for a bit, so to speak. Grabbing the one "towel" that they rationed me (now the word "towel" could not…ah, well, you know) (but it was clean at least) I used it to dry off and try to keep warm while waiting…And waiting…And—well, finally I came to the conclusion that a real shower might have to wait until the next day since I was already completely dry and since all that ever came out of the shower head was the same coughing-burping-belching-freezing-cold-water-like-substance. So I got dressed and went to eat instead; the beer would warm me up—that much I was sure of.

The next morning before the approximate crack of dawn, after a very, very, ah…well, you guessed it: cold night's sleep, I went surfing again. I walked for about fifteen minutes through some small dirt-like sand dunes to a place called Senoritas—and I had a blast. Off the lips, beautiful shear glass walls, a couple short tubes, a couple of very close calls with some rocks, but once again I was in heaven. I was wet and I was cold, but never did it enter my consciousness; I was having fun and this was how it was supposed to be. Life was good again and for those short hours coldness had no meaning for me.

At least until I got out of the water. And away from the surf. And back to the "hotel". And then along with the shower still not working, something else was still not working, and it was beginning to bug me. It hadn't worked the night before when I went to use it before going to sleep (remember I'd had a couple of beers with my dinner), and it wasn't working when I woke up to use it in the middle of the night (the beers again), and it still wasn't working when I went to use it before I went surfing at the approximate crack of dawn (this time it was the delicious dinner of fried fish and squid over rice, which unfortunately still wasn't settling correctly in my stomach, so my stomach decided not to bother with it and just moved it along). So by the time I got back from the beach, this other piece of "bathroom" furniture had about as much of this not-working-business stuff as it could stand. So it let itself be known. Throughout the whole room. And somewhat outside it too. Needless to say, I changed quite quickly and headed somewhere far away, preferably upwind, to get some sort of breakfast material that might settle my stomach a little, or at least fill it.

I ended up getting two boiled eggs, a couple of rolls, OJ, and some coffee. It wasn't what I thought I'd ordered, but at least it was good. Once again I thought to myself, "I must take another Spanish class when I get back to LA." But for that moment I was happy and full, still quite cold, but then again I wasn't hungry anymore. Umberto told me he'd check in on me at about noon to see how I was doing. Little did he know (or maybe he did know. Maybe he was a hell of a lot smarter than I gave him credit for. After all, I was the one who spent the night at the freezing beach in the heart of winter when nobody else was around except for a few straggling innkeepers, some Policia, and an occasional terrorista or left-wing rebel). So where was I? Oh, yes, little did he know that I was planning on getting the hell out of there and going someplace warm, and the quicker the better was all that mattered to me.

Since it was already close to noon I thought I'd just hang out at the "hotel". Obviously not wanting to stay in or even get near my room, which by now had gotten a very, very, very, ah…thick atmosphere to it, I ventured out into their so called courtyard to read a book and write in my journal. Now Umberto called this space a courtyard, and I was not one to doubt him, but to tell the truth there was no yard to court in to be seen. To tell the further truth, there was no grass around for miles as far as I could tell. And also a courtyard usually doesn't have laundry lines going across it. But then again this was Peru and every country has their own unique customs, so I just took the "courtyard" as one of theirs and made myself at home.

Now, you're probably wondering why I was so lackadaisical about the problem I had with my room, and why I just didn't go up to the front desk and demand that someone fix it. Well, there were many, many, many reasons, but the first and most obvious one was the fact that there wasn't a front desk—not that I could find at least. When Umberto checked me into the "hotel" the day before he just talked to the "innkeeper" (the kid) who was in the "courtyard". They talked in a very hurried Spanish, much too quick for me to understand, and the next thing I knew I was putting my bags and boards into my "room". Once again I should of suspected something when I realized that he, the "innkeeper", was in the room next to me, and a woman (a maid I thought) (and later hoped) was in the room on the other side, and that we, the three of us, were the "hotel's" only guests.

Now the night before when my shower wasn't working, the first thing I thought of was to call the front desk. But besides from the fact that there wasn't a front desk to speak of, there also wasn't a phone in my "room" to speak of to speak to this nonexistent front desk. So before my brain hurt itself I put the thought aside. Besides, I was hungry and tired, and all I wanted was some dinner and then some sleep.

On the way to dinner I asked the "innkeeper" about the shower and he assured me that it would be working in one half hour. But I was tired, remember I'd flown the entire night before, so when the other pieces of "bathroom" furniture didn't work later on in the evening, I said the hell with it and went to sleep. Besides, the atmosphere wasn't much to speak of yet. And then in the morning when that same piece of furniture still wasn't working properly, or at all for that matter, and for that matter it really did need to work, well, it was only the approximate crack of dawn, and the "innkeeper" wasn't up yet, and I wanted to go hit the surf, so I said the hell with it again, and figured the "maid" would take care of it later...

Well, later came, and later went, and still no "maid", but still quite an atmosphere. So before I settled down into the "courtyard", I found the "innkeeper" and asked him about my "bathroom" furniture and it's lack of workability. He empathized with my problem (I think that's what the translation meant) (once again a reminder for a Spanish class) and assured me that it would be working in one half hour. He assured me. So I went and I waited and I read and I wrote, knowing all the while that I would only have to delve into my room once more to grab my bags and boards—with or without its encompassing atmosphere.

And I waited...And I waited...And one o'clock lead on to two. And two o'clock lead on to three. And three o'clock lead on to me starting to get a bit hysterical. After all, I was only six or eight thousand miles away from home, in a town whose population could be counted on your left hand, waiting in a closed down "hotel" for a person I'd only met the day before, in a country where hardly anyone spoke my native tongue, and where I barely spoke theirs. But, after I calmed myself down, I knew I shouldn't be worried; I had faith. Where I found it, I'll never know. It's just like us U.S. Americans to think that no matter what we will be taken good care of—just because we're U.S. Americans.

After a bit I found a phone, the only phone in the town (in the infamous fried fish and squid over rice restaurant, which of course after the night before's bodily rejection of that meal I shied away from), and called up Umberto's house and got Romane, his maid/butler (it's my best shot at the translation), and found out that Umberto was on his way. But first a couple of stops had to be made on the way; yet he assured me Umberto would be there in half an hour. He assured me. I won't tell you about all the aggravation and anxiety I experienced while waiting the next couple of hours for my now mythical guide to show up, because you've all been there before and know the feeling. I was just hoping I wouldn't get to know this feeling too well, or too often.

Finally he showed up, and soon I was happy again. I was heading back towards Lima, towards Umberto's house, towards a rumored "real" bathroom, with rumored "real" working bathroom furniture, with rumored "real" heat, and with a rumored "real" hot shower. Less stops were made on the way back from the beach, once again I believe having to do with different hemisphere's atmospheric changes and the air flow directions going to and from the beach—or something like that.

But finally we made it to Umberto's, and finally I made it up the stairs, and finally I made it into the "real" bathroom (which Umberto assured me would have pieces of furniture that would actually work) (he assured me), and finally I made it out of my clothes, and finally I turned the shower faucet handles, and immediately I saw what I'd been hoping for, what I'd been dreaming for, what I'd by now have been willing to pay hard cash for—hot steaming water.

I felt it to make sure my eyes weren't playing tricks on me. They weren't; it was hot and I knew I'd soon be happy. Just like I am now…So let's see, how many days has it been?

Bali Reflections
Gregory Schell

> *"If the doors of perception were cleansed everything would appear to man as it is, infinite."*
>
> —William Blake

I arrived in Bali as a young twenty-three year old on April 23, 1993 with my traveling college chum Jesse. We, like many other student surfers, had saved up enough money after graduating UC Santa Barbara to travel to Indonesia. The lure of exotic, perfect waves drew Jesse and I out there ever since we were in the freshman dorms together, often daydreaming about it. At that time, Bali seemed like heaven…Perfect waves in warm tropical water with indigenous Hindu locals that were very open and friendly to foreign travelers. The island of Bali was a major stopover for anyone on the global surf trail and we felt it was the right time to go there. Our arrival in Bali had preceded the terrorist bombing of the Sari Club by about ten years.

So there I was, living out of my sleeping bag in the makeshift youth hostel in Kuta, when I was awakened by the sounds of a rooster crowing. Already I was feeling weary from the previous night's abuse of too many rum banana lassies and inhaling the Indonesian-made Djarum cloves. It was six a.m. and already the heat was stifling, on what would be our third day of the trip. Jesse and I got up and joined our Japanese surf companions, Deka and Shinsaku, for some apricot jaffles (hot pockets of apricot and peanut butter in a crusty bread shell). Collectively, we decided that today we would all eat the famous Balinese "magic mushroom" omelets, a little paranoid of what might become of us in an hour or so. Our local warung owner, Made, warned us of its powerful effects on the mind and body. The surf had gone flat (by Bali standards, it was still head high) so we concluded that this would be the right day for a mind trip.

After eating the psychedelic omelets, we loaded up the bemo with our surfboards, reggae blasting on the local radio station, and headed out for Medewi, on the Western edge of the Bakuit Peninsula, a four-hour drive from Kuta. I'm not sure at what point we all came on, but I began to hallucinate pretty intensely on all of the surroundings. Watching from the bemo's window, just blowing my mind on the Balinese countryside as it displayed it's magnificence: coconut palm trees, terraced rice fields, ornate temples and smiling Balinese people…this was a view straight out of so many Vietnam war films I had seen in film school.

Upon arriving at Medewi, we were delighted to see long left hand waves breaking over a rocky point with not a soul out. "About a six-a-foota," as Shinsaku called it. We splashed sunblock on our faces and hit the waves. We surfed for three hours non-stop in the 82-degree water. Paddling over a clear, multi-colored reef alive with crustaceans and purple sea urchins…it was brilliant. At some point, I sat up on my board and watched as Jesse slipped into a green, backlit tube…His silhouette glided in front of me and all I could do was laugh hysterically. There wasn't a water droplet out of place. All of my daydreams from school suddenly crystallized into reality. I was here in Bali, surfing in an exotic landscape, an astonishing glimpse directly taken from my dreams.

Afterward, I sat and gazed out at the Indian Ocean with salted eyebrows, a sunburnt face and a very tranquil mind. We were in a small outdoor restaurant, sipping cold coca-colas, with a slight breeze from the ocean, not saying a word. I had achieved a positively different state of mind. I began to reflect on all of the friendly local children who had literally nothing but scraps of food to eat and the tattered shirts on their backs. Yet they were all so happy. I excused myself, walked down the beach and cried. These were tears not coming from sadness, but from a major realization. I felt an intense love for all humankind. These Balinese kids were all just manifestations of myself, innocent and playful, only without the privileged background I had. It was at that moment, on the beach in Medewi, that the concept of the 'infinite' hit me. I felt the communion with any and all things around me. Blake was right. Bali had taught me a lesson, opened up a door of perception, and I could never close it again.

We arrived back in Kuta by nightfall, just in time to have nasi goreng (bits of garlic cashew chicken over steamed rice). I walked back to the warung bungalow, noticing the Southern Cross constellation above. The dark streets of Kuta were humming with the sounds of Balinese gamelan cymbals, outdoor vendors and street revelers. I settled back into my room later that night, staring at the slow moving ceiling fan…my mind exhausted but enlightened by what proved to be one of the best days of the trip so far. I never felt the need to try mushrooms again for I had experienced an intense 'Bali High' and it had transformed my life forever.

JALAMA

Mike Fraley

Years of stars fill the sky
    and cliffs return to the sand
Beaches that look like the edge of the world
    an invitation from nature to man
Waves are born on these deep ocean floors
    and grow into walls fast and clean
In the adulthood of winter these waves take new form
    and their faces are monstrous and mean
Surfers travel for many a mile
    winding their way to the shore
To slide down the face
    and escape one last tube
        this quest is what they live for
There are wind carved caves
    there's wind for days
        for kites and wind surfers to play
Securing your tent—a mandatory event
    or the wind will take it away
Now catch the last wave—pack up the camp
    Grab a burger and be on my way
But these memories of fun, and surf, and sun
    will bring me back another day
        to that magic place
        with the silent J.

The Last Secret Spot

D. J. McNamara

Keegan smiled as the Indian Summer sun warmed his cheeks and the light offshore breeze blew a scent of pine past his nose. The oar handles felt smooth in his palms as he pulled the dory through the wind ruffled water. He glanced back over his shoulder at the island and saw it was only a hundred yards further. He turned back around, facing the mainland and pulled deeper. He felt like a kid on his way to the candy store, after having found a crumpled dollar amidst the cigarette butts and broken glass littering the sidewalk. And he wasn't smiling only because of the fine weather nor for his anticipation of the waves he would soon ride but because of what Josh and Tim had said, when he'd told them he was leaving last year.

"I've had it," he'd mutter disgustedly, as they'd trudged to the van after another crowded, hostile session at the pier. He told them he was going to find a place of his own, some spot where no one had even heard of surfing! "That's the last time some kook rips me off!"

Josh had laughed. "There are no secrets left, Keeg. It's all been discovered, plundered and polluted, in the great tradition of western exploration."

Tim hadn't been so cavalier. "You can run but you can't hide. Not anymore. You gotta face it, live with it. Assimilate or perish. Just ask the Indians."

"Yeah, maybe." Keegan had replied. "But there must be some place that isn't overrun by idiots and punks yet!" He'd shaken his head to emphasize his conviction. "I just have to find it."

But inside he'd suspected they were probably right, that he just wasn't accepting reality. And that's why Keegan smiled so broadly now, his white teeth flashing in the sun. Josh and Tim, still battling hordes back home, had been wrong after all! He'd found a secret spot, up north, an island of his own where he could hide!

He'd discovered the island by accident while working for a lobster fisherman in Cold Harbor, Maine, only a month after he'd left Surf City. His original plan had been to travel up the coast, taking temporary jobs along the way, to finance an eventual Atlantic crossing to Europe where he could begin his quest. He never counted on finding what he was looking for so easily though, in Maine of all places.

The lobsterman, Ben Talbert, had hired him right away one September morning when he'd inquired about the want ad tacked to the baithouse door at the harbor. Apparently Talbert had lost his summer help, a college kid gone back to school, and was desperate that day for any able body who could assist in pulling his lobster traps out of the water.

"There's a hurr'cane comin up the coast and I got tuh haul them traps so's I don't lose them," he'd said in a thick Downeast accent.

Keegan didn't know anything about lobstering but figured it would be an interesting experience. He was also intrigued by Talbert's offer of fifty dollars just for helping him that day. It wasn't enough to get him to Europe but it would buy him a few Big Macs.

It was as they motored around to the east side of the little island where Talbert had set most of his traps, that Keegan first saw the long walled waves, sweeping around a rock point, into a small cove. It had been only two feet but the potential was obvious. And as they busily winched up lobster traps from the ocean floor his eyes kept drifting over to the tiny but perfect waves peeling along the boulder strewn shore.

Talbert noticed. "Whatcha lookin at, son?"

Keegan had nodded towards the point and replied, "The waves." Then he turned and smiled at the lobsterman. "I'm a surfer."

Talbert had stared at Keegan a moment and then turned towards the point. "I seen it pretty rough in here but I ain't never seen no surfahs."

Keegan had asked what the name of the island was.

Talbert had shrugged. "It don't have one. Hell, there's hundreds of these little rocks up and down the coast. Too much bothah namin 'em all!"

The following day the storm had come, careening through the Gulf of Maine, a hundred miles offshore. Huge surf was pushed towards Cold Harbor. The tourists were fascinated and lined the bluffs to watch the crashing waves. But Keegan had other things in mind. He persuaded Talbert to ferry him out to the island and drop him off on the lee shore which was protected from the giant swells pounding the windward side. After hiking through the pine trees on the island Keegan arrived at the cove. And as he'd suspected, and hoped, the deeper water there allowed the waves to wrap around the point just as perfectly as the day before, only much bigger. He stood in reverent silence, as eight foot walls peeled two hundred yards along the point before they finally dredged up and closed out on the rocky beach in the middle of the cove. For a moment he couldn't move. But then he screamed out loud and quickly scrambled over the rocks, punched through the shorebreak and began a long, frantic paddle to the lineup.

For three hours he rode wave after flawless, grinding wave. It was nothing at all like the beach break junk back in Surf City. The takeoff was surprisingly easy but quickly hollowed into a full bore barrel. And the first section was a harrowing, flat out race for survival. But then, after Keegan would blast out onto the shoulder, the wave slowed somewhat, allowing a full rail cutback. And Keegan would then pump and carve up and down the face, generating speed for the final, torquing tube which was every bit as fast as the first, but tighter. And as he crouched into it, and the lip poured over and around him, spinning faster and faster, he felt as it he could just keep on going forever, flying along inside an endless tube. But then, he would hear the hiss of the receding water on the beach and the rumbling of dragging rocks on the bottom and he would force himself to pull through the back of the wave before it closed out in final oblivion.

It was the finest session of his life. Not only were the waves big, powerful and perfect but best of all, he was completely alone! As far as he knew, no one had ever ridden this incredible wave. And he realized right away, after the first ride even, that he would never leave. His quest was over. He'd found his secret spot!

Indeed, Keegan hadn't left Cold Harbor. He took a job waiting tables at a restaurant in town and spent the next year surfing the waves of his unnamed island, in solitude. He figured it was better to leave the spot unidentified too, even though he'd rightfully claimed it as his. Somehow that would have spoiled everything; it would have been just another surf spot. But as long as it remained anonymous, it was still secret. After all, how could other surfers find out about a place they'd never heard of?

Keegan was still smiling as he dragged his dory up onto the west side of the island. Josh had been wrong when he'd said there were no more secrets. And Tim too. He didn't have to fight and he didn't have to join either. He would let his friends hassle it out, trying to carve their own meager niche amongst the kooks of Surf City. Keegan knew it wasn't worth it, not as long as there was one last secret spot. He hadn't sent Josh or Tim even a postcard since he'd left. He sometimes missed not having friends to share the experience with, guys who understood what it was all about. But he knew if he told even one person it would all be ruined. He'd seen it before. No, he was better off alone.

Keegan chuckled as he lifted his board from the dory. Sure, it was lonely, playing the role of the last solitary surfer. "But someone's gotta do it!" he snickered aloud.

Before he emerged from the woods, though, Keegan heard something which chilled his spine, like an icy trickle seeping through the neck seal of a wetsuit. He stiffened and listened closer. At first he heard only the wind rustled pines and maybe the faint roar of the surf in the distance. But then, there it was again, that all too familiar sound of a long, shrill, hoot!

"No fuckin way!" Keegan muttered as he began running towards the cove. It couldn't be! It had to be a trick of the wind.

But as he burst from the woods onto the rocky beach, his beach, he saw it was true! There, anchored in the cove was a large sloop. And squaring off the bottom of the four foot wall shifting around the point was a yellow wetsuited surfer. And as he watched the surfer slash off the top, sending a huge fan of spray above the lip, Keegan heard it again. Three other neon suited surfers in the channel hooted and cheered like fraternity house drunks.

Keegan felt a knifing pain in his chest and almost dropped his board. Then, as the yellow surfer emerged from the tube, both fists raised, he heard another voice, this one on the shore.

"YEAH!"

Keegan turned his eyes down the beach. The guy had his back to him but it didn't matter. Keegan had seen his picture before, in the magazines. And as he stared in disbelief, the guy wheeled around his bazooka sized Nikon lens and aimed it at the orange suited surfer, dropping into the six footer off the point.

The Last Wave
Max Montgomery

Numerous spats, breakups and divorces have been caused waiting for one. People have been late for work and lost jobs because of this. School going surfers have no doubt spent hundreds of hours in detention hall due to this. It will happen to you the next time you surf, and there is nothing you can do to prevent it. Yes, indeed, I'm talking about waiting for the dreaded next wave in.

The infamous next wave in is a very important part of surfing because it is the main link to the last surf session. It is what is relived during the walk to the car and what is remembered on the way home, therefore, it must be a good wave. Getting this next wave in often turns into a Catch-22 situation as the wave in will end up being so good it rekindles the stoke to stay out and get more, or it will end up being so bad that one must stay out and catch another to save face. Caught in this pickle countless times, I have surfed myself way past dark in seemingly never ending sessions. One can never paddle in, of course, that is the ultimate disgrace.

A special attitude is adopted by those seeking the next wave in. Some people actually announce the fact that they are going in, hoping that fellow surfers will let them catch the next wave in to reduce the crowd. This doesn't work too well. What usually happens is a modification of surf etiquette. A great deal of surfers actually think it is ok to drop in on someone if it is to be their next wave in. "But dude, I was like going in…"

A few weeks ago I was in Hawaii and was out at Lanieakea with my friend Buddy. Although the waves weren't great they were much better than anything we'd been surfing the past week. After a few waves Buddy went in. Since he had the car keys I began worrying about having to walk home. Bummed to end the surf session so early I started looking for that ride to shore. Begrudgingly I caught a poor wave in only to find him in the car happily reading the paper. Being undergunned he was content with the waves he'd caught and, being the perfect host, he had planned to patiently wait for me as long as necessary.

Today I was freezing my butt off in the cold waters of Santa Cruz; I had got a couple of tubes, but it was not at all like the epic session I had yesterday. Only 4 guys were out, but the waves were few and far between, in fact, two surfers would have been capacity for the day. The tide was starting to turn and the waves had been as infrequent as a 51 day swell. It was near dark and I had to get going. Looking seaward it was calm as a lake. Although I'm not religious I was exploring all avenues for a wave in. Looking skyward I said four Hail Mary's; I even got on my hands and knees and prayed to J.C. himself, which is pretty hard to do on a short board. Covering all bases, I switched to Eastern religion and chanted a "Pleeeze send a wave" mantra over and over. Something worked as a set came from nowhere. I managed to get into the first wave but came too hard off the bottom and wasn't able to stall in the pocket. Of course I couldn't leave. Paddling back to the line up I told myself and anyone listening up above that the last wave didn't really count as it was not quite good enough. I had wanted a tube, and I would go in on the next wave, really I would.

There was a lull of eternity before another set came. I let the first one go, dropped in on the second and pulled into one of the longest barrels of my life. Kicking out, I sat there deciding what to do. For a few seconds it was touch and go, but, counting my blessings, I went in. After all, it was one hell of a wave.

Bios

JOHN CARMONA has been surfing for about nine years. He learned to surf at Marine Street in Manhattan Beach. He rides Oak Surfboards shaped by Wayne Okamoto; his favorite breaks are Back Yards Sunset, Playa Hermosa (Costa Rica), 9 Palms (Cabo San Lucas), Oxnard Shores, Del Mar, and, of course, Marine Street. He writes, "Nothing in this visible world can compare to the great feeling of surfing and being part of nature."

SEBASTIAN DEBOVIAN grew up surfing Newport and Huntington Beach after the short board revolution. His search for waves took him all along the West Coast and down in deepest Mexico. No job, class or commitment could keep him out of the water when there was a swell hitting the coast. "If you love the ocean, give something back. Join the Surfrider Foundation." On May 31, 1993, Debovian (whose real name was William Shadden) was shot and killed during a robbery attempt. He was a great poet and a great man, and is missed by all who knew him.

TERRENCE E. DUNN first surfed in fourth grade. "I placed my feet upon the sticky wet surface of the long board, the wave picked me up from behind, it carried me for a few seconds, then I fell. The feeling hasn't changed since. My favorite spots are mainly days in my head; rides that will last up there forever. Some took place in Boca Borranca, Costa Rica or Herradura, Peru or 56th Street in Newport, and others are just daydreams which help me pass through the ride of everyday life. Since *Paper Shredders* was first published, I have written and published three novels, gotten married, had a daughter, and surfed a lot. (Although, as a true surfer, I have to ask, 'Is a lot ever enough?')"

MIKE FRALEY started surfing twenty years ago in Huntington Beach. He surfs competitively as a amateur, and was #1 Master in California in the 1985 WSA. He competes less these days because he has two small boys and they take priority. He rides Channel Islands surfboards, and his favorite spots are the rights at Mussel Shoals and the left off Tarantulas Point "Jalama" of course.

CHARLENE GOLDMAN writes "When my husband goes out surfing he comes home with more blueness in his eyes. That's all I really know about surfing. For now, that's enough." Her husband, Dennis, rides a 7 1/2 foot Canyon mini-longboard tri-fin, and surfs mostly at Tourmaline in Pacific Beach.

JOHN W. HART III claims he was the best body surfer in Beverly Hills High School. He bodysurfed every day every summer from when he was 8 until he was 18. An early proponent of blue water bodysurfing, his technique earned him the nickname "The Rock"

DON HURZELER started surfing at age nine. His first board was a Reynold Yater (the seventh board he made). His current board is a six foot two inch twin fin made by David Nuuhiuia. Since he now lives in Inverness, Illinois...near Chicago...his surfing is limited to a few times a year in California and a week or two in Hawaii. He is President for Life of the Inverness Surf Club. His favorite break is the Huntington Beach Pier when it is big and not crowded, like after a nuclear attack or during a deadly outbreak of swine flu.

KEVIN JOY has been playing in the water all his life: body surfing, riding the blue mats at Huntington, kneeriding, and even bodyboarding. Now approaching mid-fifties, he plans to try standing up sometime soon. He rides a fifteen year old Sunset kneeboard shaped by Tim Bessell. He has surfed various breaks from north of San Francisco to Baja, and does not get in the water often enough.

RYAN KORINKE has been bodyboarding for four years. He rides Mike Stewart Turbos, and his favorite breaks are Salt Creek and Sleepy Hollow. He was inspired to write surf poetry by the power of the waves, and the "no fear attitude when you drop into a wave or a shallow reef."

STEPHEN F. KRAFT—former pier rat, member of the Generation X car crash set. His favorite wave is Sri Lanka Reef, Bali. He surfs a Contra 6'8". His favorite quote is "Always leave them hating you."—Steve Powers.

D.J. MCNAMARA became a surfer when he first saw *Endless Summer* in 1965, although he didn't catch his first wave until 1974, at the age of 15. After all those years of waiting, he stood up and rode all the way in on that first wave. Thirty years and three kids later, he is still as stoked as ever. His home break is The Rivermouth, in Ogunquit, Maine, "a long righthand, miniature reverse Mundacca". When not surfing, he shapes and glasses boards under his own "Shed Shapes" label, coaches soccer, and writes both fiction and non-fiction. Currently he is working on a novel about a hermit surfer who lives on a small mountain near the coast of Maine.

ROBERT MEYER learned to surf from his uncles at the age of seven. He surfed weekends in Santa Monica and summers in Newport. He moved to Napa when he was a freshman in high school, and, due to the two hour drive to the beach, has not been able to surf near as much as he would like since. His favorite spot is Stinson Beach, which is not as harsh as Ocean Beach. His favorite boards are "any good deal."

MAURO MONTEIRO—Virgo, Angeleno, transplant from Rio de Janeiro, Brazil, a self taught flowist of spoken swells considers waves to have similar qualities as poems read out loud. They are both gone in a flash yet seem to linger and remain in memory when their impacts are felt. Monteiro considers waves as being a constant form of enjoyment whether body surfing, belly boarding, and even when stand up surfing on Styrofoam boards acquired at the local department store as young grom. Formative years (mid to late Seventies through early Eighties) spent scouring Southern California for skateable terrain, hiking up for runs (before resorts allowed boards) at Mt. Pinos on prototype snowboards, and glass-off sessions and dawn patrols at Zuma, Leo Carillo, Staircase, and County Line (ok, Malibu, El Porto, and Jalama to change it up some). Blessings to Yemanja. Keep your beaches clean.

MAX MONTGOMERY has been surfing since the summer of 1979. As a self-employed computer consultant, he manages to work as little as possible and surf as much as possible. His favorite spots are Natural Bridges, Three Mile and Getchel Street in Santa Cruz and Velzyland in Hawaii. He rides a deep channeled 6'8" Pearson Arrow thruster shaped by Bob Pearson. When it is large he breaks out his 7'4" Byrning Spear shaped by the master of deep channels himself—Alan Byrne. Now and then he goes long boarding on an ancient 10'2" tanker from Len Dibben in Western Australia.

STEPHANIE MOOD writes "My surfer husband, John, inspired "Elementary". When he comes home from surfing, his aura is filled with the liquid energy of light and color. We both started surfing on rubber mats in '74 when we moved to San Diego. We graduated to boogie boards, but John kept catching bigger & bigger waves, while I stayed closer to the shore. We live at the beach & don't plan to move very far away—ever." Stephanie teaches English and Creative Writing at Grossmont College.

JOHN MORITZ has been surfing for 43 years. He learned to surf at Seal Beach, at the Pee Hole. He likes to surf with his wife at San Onofre. His favorite surf spots are Boneyard and Malibu. He is currently semi-retired, and enjoys short surf trips and long rides on small waves.

BOB MOSELEY has been surfing for 15 years. For the past few years he has ridden Fluid Express Surfboards shaped by Mike Hudnall. He enjoys surfing the Outer Banks of North Carolina and the Bahamas, but his favorite break is St Augustine's Blowhole. "In peak conditions, Blowhole offers lone, down the line tubes and steep drops.

C. MULROONEY lives in Pasadena. We're not sure where he surfs.

RICHARD NESTER writes "When I was younger, I used to run every morning near the mouth of the Santa Ana River. Every morning I would see surfers, shivering in the winter cold, climbing into wet suits, pulling boards from dilapidated vans. I held a stereotype of surfers as worthless lay-abouts who only came out when the sun shined. I quickly saw how wrong I was. These dudes were serious! Surfers, like poets, seemed both on the edge of society and at the center of a grand, wonderful passion. There particular surfers looked high school age, and I wondered if their parents and teachers could ever appreciate the dedication needed to be a surf bum."

BRYCE SAIDENBERG will go anywhere, try anything, meet anyone, ride any board for the sake of surfing. He's a maniac. He only wants to go everywhere, do everything, meet everyone, and ride every wave. Good luck to him.

GREGORY SCHELL has been an avid surfer ever since he could drive himself to the beach. His favorite spots are Hammond's Reef in Santa Barbara, Olo Walu in Maui, and Malibu Surfrider in Los Angeles. His surfboards are shaped by Dev Gregory. "Surfing has always been a kind of spiritual salvation for me, a chance to become one with the planet."

ZACK SHERERTZ has been surfing for five and a half years. He rides Rock Shapes (shaped by Rick Rock in San Clemente). His favorite surf spots are Popotla in Baja California, Churches on Camp Pendleton, and Waiohai on Kauai. He is a member of the San Onofre Surf Club, and has a passion for travel, especially when surfing is involved.

LAWRENCE SCHULZ lives, writes and surfs in Huntington Beach. His poems have appeared in both regional and national anthologies. He is the author of four books of poems including *American Streets, Say It Strong, Season of the River*, and *We Surf*. He also has one spoken word CD entitled *Spoken Songs*. He is currently working on a collection of short stories about Orange County.

WARD SMITH, who lives on 10 acres in the Santa Cruz Mountains, started surfing in the summer of 1961. He is an avid surfer who has lived and surfed in Santa Cruz County for the past 30 years where he still surfs 3 to 4 days each week. As a goofy foot his favorite surf spots are Pakalas on Kauai and Restaurants on Tavarua. He has written one book (*Gemcutting A Lapidary Handbook*), worked on another both writing and researching (*200 Years of Surfing Literature*) which was just published, wrote the foreword for the *The Surfin'ary*, and has written numerous articles for a variety of surfing and non surfing magazines. Finally, he has a collection of 1255 books on surfing.

CHRISTINE TRZYNA grew up in the coal-filled woodlands of Western Pennsylvania. The first waves she encountered were at "Chautauqua on the Lake" Erie. She vacationed at the Atlantic later off the coasts of Jersey, Maryland, and Virginia. Now a California "native", her surf poetry is inspired by the beaches from Paradise to Dume Coves, west of Malibu. She does not presently surf, but loves the action.

About the Editors

GARY WRIGHT has been surfing for over thirty years, in California as well as Hawaii, Fiji, Tahiti, Tonga, Bali, Sumatra, mainland Mexico, Baja and Costa Rica. As president and founder of Killer Dana Inc., he is active in the surfing community as both a retailer and a patron of the arts. He has an extensive library of historic surfing literature, an eclectic mix of original surf art, and a collection of rare and unique vintage surfboards, many of which he still rides on occasion.

Mr. Wright lives in Dana Point, California. He is a goofyfoot, which may help explain some things. When not out surfing, he enjoys reading, writing, and above all traveling toward the next perfect wave.

G. MURRAY THOMAS has performed his poetry all over Southern California, at almost every major poetry venue. He has also performed at Lollapalooza, The Whiskey, The Coach House and the 1996 National Poetry Slam.

Thomas' first full length collection of poems, *Cows on the Freeway*, was published by iUniverse in 2000. He has also published five chapbooks, *Death to the Real World, Opposite Oceans, Poetry Spilled All Over the Carpe, A Rare Thing*, and *Songs of Inappropriate Desire*.

His latest project is MURRAY, a garage jazz/spoken word band. In MURRAY, Thomas performs his poetry over improvised musical backing.

My very first wave
I took off late
Looked both ways
Then went straight

By the sound of his voice
I'd pretty much bet
That the guy I hopped
Was pretty upset

Was first his rail
And then his fin
That took out my ankle
And half my shin

978-0-595-35131-2
0-595-35131-X

Printed in the United States
33441LVS00005B/238-285